Relentless

Relentless

Pressing through the Storms of Life

NATHANIEL SANDERSON

RESOURCE *Publications* • Eugene, Oregon

RELENTLESS
Pressing through the Storms of Life

Copyright © 2021 Nathaniel Sanderson. All rights reserved. Except for brief quotations in critical publications or reviews, no part of this book may be reproduced in any manner without prior written permission from the publisher. Write: Permissions, Wipf and Stock Publishers, 199 W. 8th Ave., Suite 3, Eugene, OR 97401.

Resource Publications
An Imprint of Wipf and Stock Publishers
199 W. 8th Ave., Suite 3
Eugene, OR 97401

www.wipfandstock.com

PAPERBACK ISBN: 978-1-6667-1204-9
HARDCOVER ISBN: 978-1-6667-1205-6
EBOOK ISBN: 978-1-6667-1206-3

JULY 30, 2021

For Arik and Grace, who never gave up on me,
even in the deepest throes of my PTSD.

Contents

Preface | vii

Warm Fuzzies | 1
Wow | 2
Aristotle | 3
We Really Need to See a Therapist | 4
Did I Lose My Poetry? | 5
Peace | 6
Peace 2 | 7
Nightmares | 8
The Giant Asp | 9
Am I Enough | 10
Isolation | 11
Lost | 12
Habits | 13
Lonely | 14
The Deep Loneliness | 15
Inspired Again | 17
Feeling Betrayed | 18
The Dichotomy | 20
Unworthy | 23
Freedom in Death | 24
Best Friend | 26

Twenty Years | 29
Peace Like a River | 30
Fear and Anxiety | 31
The Awakening | 34
The Missing Link | 36
My Dilemma | 37
Rebirth in Moonlight | 39
Chapter 27: Peace | 41
The New, But Old Dilemma | 42
The Confrontation | 44
This isn't Over | 46
Re-evaluating Joy | 48
Why Joy Has Been Distant | 49
Time and Space | 51
Forgiveness | 52
Hunter | 53
Crisis Fatigue | 54
Breaking My Habits | 55
The Oncoming Storm | 56
Relief | 58
Processing Conflict | 59
The Depth of Struggle | 60
Balking At Danger | 61
A Shame | 62
Such a Shame | 63
The Abusive Cycle | 64
The Road Ahead | 66
The Kindling of Hope | 67
The Burden I Bear | 68
The Harmony | 69
Resilient and in Command | 70
Have I Dwelt Too Long? | 72

The Betrayal | 73
Beyond the Veil | 74
The Molten Being | 75
The Passing Storm | 76
Seizing my Destiny | 77
I want to be more | 78
Relentless | 79

Preface

2020 WAS A TOUGH year, I don't think anyone will ague that. I had such high hopes for it, though. I figured I couldn't let the pandemic stop me from achieving at least some of my goals. So I kept at it: I got my book, *Resilient*, published; I got full-time hours at my job as a therapist; and I finally built a healthy lifestyle after years of failed attempts.

I found that, through all the storms of 2020, the best thing to do was to keep on keeping on. Easier said than done, trust me. I have ADHD, which means things like filling in forms or formatting manuscripts is prohibitively difficult. Add a pandemic to the mix and you have a perfect storm for someone to justifiably take a step back. I didn't walk away though; I kept my head up and leaned on that new, healthy lifestyle.

There were days I wanted to give in, and there were more that I did just give in and do nothing. The trick was getting back up at the end of it all and not holding it against myself that I couldn't get going the day before. I learned to show such kindness to myself. So much so that even looking back on my old poetry and seeing how much self-hate I still fostered now hurts. I was pretty hard on my past self, despite him not being equipped for the cruel world that we live in.

I guess what I'm trying to say is this: you are worth it. Easily said, hard to believe. 2020 taught me that lesson in so many ruthless ways, and through it I learned to be Relentless. I became this inevitable force in 2020, and it carried me through such a difficult season. In these pages, I chronicle my journey through the pandemic as I discovered how to finally remove the shackles of self-hate from my life. To do so, I had to face what is possibly the hardest truth about me. I had to face my deepest shame.

I considered not including this in here, and even in writing it I am not convinced I am ready to have it out in the world. It is important though, to this story, to give context to who I am at my core. For a decade, I was sexually abused. From the ages of six to sixteen, before it suddenly stopped. The memories haunted me for years, until this past summer when I finally started to talk about it. With the help of what can only be described as a legendary tier therapist, I was able to come to terms with it. No easy task.

Since embracing the scars on my soul and the pain in my heart, my life has improved significantly. Going to the source of most of my shame, self-hatred, and sorrow, and giving it space to heal has been a difficult but healing journey. I have come a long way in the short months since that process began. I understand my anxiety and my fear so much better now that I have discovered this place of love and understanding of my scars.

As I am more than the sum total of my scars, so too are you reading this. The burdens you bear need not be yours alone. Therapy is where I finally found the peace I've sought for so many years. What you've been through and what was done to you does not define you beyond that which you allow it to. The journey to finding that peace is through therapy. It is not easy. It is not fast. You will see the depths of the darkness in your soul and everything you may hate about yourself in the process; I promise you that all of that pain is worth it in the end. Do not give in to the narrative that you are nothing more than your scars. Believe that you are more. Believe and find help, even if you think you don't need it, as it may be the difference you need.

Now, all that said, 2020 was still a tough year. I lost many friends, and not even to the pandemic; they chose to leave my life. The one hard thing to remember about growth is that there will be people who do not like who you become. Do not let that stop you from growing. Health is more important than people who demand you remain in bondage to your trauma. Just as you learn who you are beyond your scars, the people in your life will need to learn who you are as you change and grow and embrace this new life you've chosen.

WARM FUZZIES

To be told that I am a good therapist,
What a world I live in.
For so long I was lost in the mist,
But now I am helping others lost therein!
What a surreal change of pace,
And yet I am equal to the task.
I don't even have to put on a good face,
Because it is in the sun that I now bask!
God, I've made such a good life,
A life free of my old strife.

WOW

I suppose I knew that it would happen eventually,
That the last dregs of my imposter would leave.
I just didn't expect it to happen actually,
And the feeling; you would not believe.

ARISTOTLE

I seek the freedom alcohol brings,
Such that we could have a little fun.
Many lessons we learned in our springs,
But now there remains mischief undone.
Aristotle is my name,
But as of yet you leave me a stranger.
Fear not, for it is for your health that I come.
I bring freedom from this stoic ranger,
We shall speak more this weekend,
As your soul continues on the mend.

WE REALLY NEED TO SEE A THERAPIST

My thoughts wander again,
Focus lost in this fen.
I try to work,
But my thoughts seem to shirk.
It's not that I'm unhappy.
It's not that I feel crappy.
I just can't seem to focus,
And my thoughts are like many locusts.
I just want an open ear,
Without any need to fear.
Let's put on the list,
A nice visit to a therapist.

DID I LOSE MY POETRY?

I find myself lost and alone,
Not that I'm lonely either,
Just that my soul lacks a tone.
I don't want my poetry to wither,
There's a fog like a loud moan,
And it chokes me like a tether.
I just can't seem to escape this fug,
How I wish to be free.
Moments ago, I was so smug,
My brain was quite lively,
But now it is just an empty mug.
What did I do to lose my poetry?

PEACE

I find myself quite at peace,
It's weird.
It seems I've opened life's lease,
Then steered.
I made the world my own,
It's nice.
I start a year no longer alone,
No vice.
So, I guess what I'm trying to say,
Oddly,
Is that I've finally found my way.
I'm free.

PEACE 2

I look upon this life I have built,
And wonder how I ever got here.
Peace flows through me, clearing the silt,
Lending me strength to lend my ear.
The garden I now tend is beautiful.
Sprouts of a new life bloom,
And while the garden is by no means yet full,
The bright sun casts out all the old gloom.

NIGHTMARES

I am often haunted by monsters,
Although I've never seen one out of human flesh.
Why then is it fear that my brain fosters?
Why then, am I caught in the clutches of its mesh?
I am beyond equal to this task,
As one, I will rise again from the dust.
I will drink once more from life's flask,
And proudly bear my rust.
I am the Fury in the Night,
I am the Light of the Dawn.
I am the Hunter out of Sight,
And the Gentle Fawn.
It is my voice that calls out in the darkness,
It is my will that shrugs of these chains.
It is my life that bucks in the harness,
It is my soul that is scarred by these pains!
There is no one who can stop me,
I will not be kept from my destiny.
There is no chance I will hide,
My destiny is too great to be denied.
I will rise,
Right before your eyes.

THE GIANT ASP

What I seek is forever on the horizon,
It ever eludes my grasp.
It's something I haven't even laid my eyes on,
For all I know it could be a giant asp.
Although, truth be told, it should be cool,
But like, I've so often been made the fool.
I guess I'm just gun-shy.
I know I like to reach high,
And I've already moved forward.
My destiny will not be denied,
The die is cast and this life is moving onward.
My destiny is now a thing from which I cannot hide.

AM I ENOUGH

Am I enough?
I often wonder this in the quiet hours.
My heart and soul have had it rough,
Which has made it hard to stop and smell the flowers.
I want to think that I am,
But I worry.
I worry about being some niche man
A great idea beloved by the snobby,
But despised by the masses in secret.
It seems I am too much,
As often when I open up, people throw a fit.
I wasn't always as such,
But I didn't always share who I was.
Where now, I share who I am all the time.
I wish I created a buzz,
Instead of fearing being seen as slime.
Now I worry if that makes me vain,
Even though I only seek validation that I am not a stain.

ISOLATION

I will not lose myself to this isolation.
I may be locked in this home alone,
But I will not be lost to the desolation.
My heart will not turn to stone.
See, while my loved ones may not be near,
And the world is filled with a growing hysteria,
I am not truly alone here.
I get to be digitally connected to the area.
While my soul yearns for connection,
My heart remains full. That is how we will survive this pandemic's selection,
By staying home and leaving the outside world to the gull.

LOST

When the words smoothly flow,
And you are lost to their rapture,
I could say that that is when you know.
Fresh coffee cools as the book, I cannot stow,
My full attention, the words did capture.
It's by this point that if you didn't already know,
I'll tell you beyond a shadow of a doubt,
What you are reading is a treasure.

HABITS

Getting in the habit of writing every day,
It's tough, but we all start somewhere.
Even if it's a restart today,
Every little bit helps you to care.

It has taken me some time,
But I have risen to my feet.
I'm getting back into the rhyme,
I might be down but I ain't beat.

LONELY

I feel like sometimes I am a lonely rock,
On the shore of a churning sea.
I look at my life and take stock,
Roiling breakers are all I see.
It's not that I don't have support,
For as the tides lowers, I am no longer alone.
It's that I see these pairs as they all cavort,
I stand without a partner in my zone.
I struggle as I am told to settle,
Find a pretty girl alone out there,
I could find one who doesn't test my mettle,
But to my future self that wouldn't be fair.
So, I guess all this to say,
That I feel quite lonely today

THE DEEP LONELINESS

It is in the quiet hours that my loneliness arrives.
The subtle yearning for another seeps into my soul,
Filling it as bees fill their hives.
It is beginning to take its toll.
It grows louder as I clear time for me,
It makes it hard to look inward.
What does it not want me to see?
What does it not want dragged forward?
It seems to fill my mind,
Silencing my many voices.
What is there to find,
That has so inhibited my choices?
What lies there in the depths,
That feels it cannot speak?
What has drowned out even my wrath?
What is it that I seek?
Do I need more time with my loved ones?
Do I need one who enjoys walks in the sun?
Do I need to finish my priorities?
Show me what it is I do not see.

Should I stand up to this treatment,
And rest in the new space?
Should my Anxiety meet the team and show her face?
Share her so she no longer fears our commitment?
Let us meet again in the morning,
Sleep on it and enjoy the evening.

INSPIRED AGAIN

I would describe this season as tough,
Given the state if the world.
Good thing I've crawled out of the rough.
My soul, once more, is unfurled.
I feel like, once more, I will do well.
Not that I was doing all that badly,
It's just that I feel swell,
And feeling good helps me to work gladly.
As I feel my life anew,
Look out because I am coming for you too.

FEELING BETRAYED

I knew where this road would lead,
As death and ash litter the ground beneath my feet.
Still, I did not expect an ally to hurt one in need.
Still, I did not expect to see this kind of defeat.
I thought we stood as one against evil,
My allies and I advocating for the weak.
Yet here I stand surrounded by weevils,
As this alliance collapses as I speak.
Why is it that such acts go unpunished?
How could one so trained ignore the broken?
This life I thought had flourished,
Dies in the way that is unspoken.
While I am not alone, I feel Fury,
While I am not undone, I feel Agony.
I brought forth a solution in a hurry,
Which the powers that be found all sunny.
Still, I am reeling.
Still, I am shocked.
There is enough pain that this world is feeling,
That we should not be the ones it rocked.
We are made to be a safe haven,
We are trained to be quite a maven,
Yet even we falter.
Even we fail.

It is not enough though to give in,
I will rise again ready to begin.
I will not be deterred by this sin,
The world will change by my avail.

THE DICHOTOMY

Let's ask a simple question that has a simple answer:
Should our shared history matter?
I don't think anyone would argue that this is a hard question sir,
And yet it is the only one on the platter.
I often feel it unfair to call on the past,
Especially given how you've grown.
Yet nothing I do seems to last.
I feel out of solutions and done.
I may receive your love often enough,
But that doesn't make up for you dismissing me.
I will not deny that your life has been rough,
I would merely ask that you stop punching me.
I am baffled that I have to bring that up,
That after all we have been through,
You seem to refuse my cup.
That after spending so long as one crew,
You would treat me like the one who defiled you.
After the dust settled, who was with you?
After all the storms and the mess, who was with you?
When your own mother rejected you, who was with you?
When the institution allowed visits, who was with you?
When the community persecuted you, who defended you?
When the city ostracized you, who defended you?
When you had to leave quickly, who moved you?

When you were in pain, who comforted you?
Every one of these questions has but one solution.
It wasn't some grand coalition,
No, it was one man who saw you through the desolation.
Why then?
Why must I even write this refrain?
Why must I suffer at your hands?
Why must I be treated as a stain?
What does it take to be welcome in your lands?
Clearly being consistent doesn't do the trick!
Clearly caring matters not one bit!
Perhaps the solution is sucking your dick,
As your partners get to easily fit.
Seems like you welcome them and not I,
Despite the years of history.
She gets to live while I must die.
My friend this is quite the mystery,
Now, I'm happy you've found someone,
That's not what pisses me off.
No, no, what has led me to being done,
Is that I proffer ideas and you dismiss them and scoff.
All while her ideas get treated like gold,
I get treated like your abuser,
While our history lies ignored and old.
You break your back to amuse her,
While tossing me in the trash.
I want a deep friendship with you man,
But I keep getting treated like a bad rash.
You say all the right things but your actions fall painfully silent.

I feel like you'd die for your partner,
And sooner trade my life for hers.
I am sick and tired of being a punching bag,
While the only people you treat well are the ones you shag.

UNWORTHY

The cacophony of nature echoes around me,
As machinery drones in the background.
The memories of unworthiness accusing silently.
Do I deserve kindness as my rage abounds?
The question haunts my steps,
All while the world continues to turn.
Futility tears my heart out like forceps,
As my fire can't seem to get this wood to burn.
How can I make an impact?
When my woes hold me so fast.
How then, can I make it through intact,
And create a community that lasts?
I feel I am a slave to my own emotion,
As it is heightened by medication.
Although a loved one was caught in a commotion,
Hurt by another loved one, I went over my quotient.
As my Rage has been heard,
And its echoes felt,
I believe the next step is inferred,
I go to make stony hearts melt.
Now that my picture is full, wide and clear,
I will step into the arena with words for all to hear.

FREEDOM IN DEATH

I once feared Death so greatly,
And believed any who claimed to ease that fear.
That path led me to be hateful and stately,
And even as I learned and grew, hate held my ear.
It was subtle, as I thought I followed love,
Yet all around me was judgement and hate.
I thought I could change the world for one up above,
While surrounded by those fearing their inevitable fate.
They let the fear of Death blind them,
And when confronted with the Truth, they ran.
It wasn't until I met Death that my own fear began to stem,
And it wasn't until I removed my blinders that my life truly began.
For a time, I thought Death now feared me,
Twice we met and twice I emerged victorious.
Yet in our most recent meeting I truly began to see,
People often describe Death as glorious.
I've been dissuaded of that notion.
See, Death and I caused quite a commotion,
When we met the first time I really began to fear,
And our second meeting I went to him in tears.
His is an embrace of peace,
Solace for the weary soul.
Yet rather than hasten the closing of life's lease,

He only takes those who can no longer afford its toll.
There is nothing to fear in Death,
As it is when we finally get our eternal rest.
Not that we should hurry to our last breath,
But that we should enjoy our time here and make it the best.
It is in this new understanding that I am free,
And through it all, I will now be a force of love.
My life will be like a tree,
Slow to start, yet growing to shade all from branches above.
There will be rest in my company,
For all who are willing I will be a guide,
Forever moving forward from my strife.
For all who feel that they are locked outside,
I vow to leave the door open into my life.
If Death isn't to be feared and there is no overarching reason,
Then to choose your own destiny is your purpose.
Those are the rules of my house, yet to disobey is not treason,
That is to say, life is what you make it and only you can choose to go beyond the surface.

BEST FRIEND

So many thoughts fill my mind,
It is difficult to organize.
I hunt diligently for thoughts that are kind,
Yet wrath and disappointment fill my eyes.
See, I hurt at the loss of a brother,
Even the mere thought.
My feelings I've often had to smother,
Finding often that his love had to be bought.
I suppose I am also baffled,
Yet not at the same time.
I feel that so rarely events can be raffled,
And I see everything, so sublime.
It is difficult to ignore the truth,
And so often I have done just that.
I feel it so keenly like a pain in a tooth,
Every time I don't step up to bat.
I regularly chose him over others,
Just to be ditched at the wayside.
I am tired of compromising my values to be brothers.
I want people who actively choose to be at my side.
This feels like it was a long time coming,
That my strength of character can no longer waiver.
Especially when my values have come into questioning.
I will not give ground when it comes to making community safer.

I can no longer abide those dear to me self-harming,
Especially when I have a way to make it better.
Years I have toiled in this soil,
Just to have it go unnoticed.
Friendship shouldn't feel like water to oil,
Yet to not have my work at all noticed?
More than that, to have it written off?
To have it be the object of scoff?
How foolish do you have to be?
How can I toil and you not see?
So much work over so many years,
And you choose now to weaponize your tears?
I built this thing you called an accident,
And I assure you that there was precedent.
This community has grown closer over many deep chats,
Held intentionally with many at bats.
The yield you see springing from this ground,
Is a direct result of my toil.
No matter how much you search around,
This flourishing community lies within my soul.
I feel insulted.
I feel hurt.
I feel unseen.
I feel devalued.
I feel unwanted.
I feel discarded.
While my soul may be at peace,
It seems you are coming up on your lease,
And the loudest thing I feel is disappointment.
After such a long friendship, how is that my statement?
Yet it seems the choice is out of my hands,
My love met with steeper and steeper demands,

While that same love is called into question.
How about our long history, when does that get a mention?
Long after the fact when the dust is settling.
Discarded in the heat of the moment,
As though it is but a tool for meddling.
Used to draw me out of my settlement.
Where is the trust drawn from those years?
Where is the trust implicated in your tears?
Would I not have your best interests at heart?
When have I done actions for your ill?
When did my words start meaning less than the start?
All these years and yet you do not trust me still.
Sure, you trust me in the day to day,
And yet as it bleeds into something at all hard,
Suddenly I have nothing of value to say?
You wield our history like a trump card,
Yet when the rubber meets the road, you ignore it.
Forever choosing your partner over me.
While expecting me to bow to you like a git.
It's not that your perspective is one I cannot see,
It's that what I say doesn't seem to matter to you
It feels like you don't see me for who I am.
It's like you see me as water when I am glue,
And you see my intentions as a big scam.
So long in our friendship I have allowed you to hurt me,
Accepting you and your trauma together.
I'm done being hurt and I'm done watching you hurt yourself, see,
I love you dearly and I want your life to be better.
I absolutely do not want to stop being brothers,
But I can no longer abide you and your partner choosing your trauma over others.

TWENTY YEARS

Just a disappointing waste.
Honestly,
Twenty years thrown away in haste.
Messily.
I fully understand what went down,
I hate it.
Broken reasoning built in Traumatown.
What a fit.
Now I have to wait and see the echoes.
Disappointing.
What more have I lost in these thoughtless throes?
Something.
I would rather this didn't make sense,
At least then I would be sad and not building this fence.
But there are some fights you just can't win,
And you still step into the arena when your values are challenged within.

PEACE LIKE A RIVER

Sadness is quite the companion.
Beyond that, tears are so freeing.
Such a controversial opinion,
Yet still there is solace for the soul that stops fleeing.
I find crying to be like a walk by a river,
Calming, peaceful, healing, and low-key unpleasant.
Yet I am rewarded when I ignore my discomfort and just give 'er.
My soul cried when pain comes, just like a pheasant,
And even still, it is good.
In tears, there is vulnerability.
In tears, there is growth ability.
In tears, you can tell more than you normally would.
It is as though tears are the soul's food.
There when there is pain.
There when you notice a stain.
There even when you are not in the mood.
There is freedom in tears.
Everyone should cry, no matter their fears.

FEAR AND ANXIETY

My chest feels cold.
My hands are shaky.
I ask the questions of old;
Am I flaky?
Am I enough?
Am I too much?
I don't feel tough,
And it is not usually as such.
I guess I am afraid,
As even writing this stresses me out.
My nerves are frayed.
I don't know if I can survive this bout.
Well, let's look at the facts:
See, I've survived every fight thus far,
And 'tis is no different in the way it acts.
Why here, am I afraid of not making the bar?
Is it that my humanity was removed?
Is this also why I am relieved?
I think I need this fear to be moved.
My Fear and Anxiety are never believed.
I praise them in others,
Yet discard them in me.
It is loud and it smothers.
And it feels like not a person.

She knows she is free,
And to be free is to be hit with reason.
Reason is by no means bad,
It is just so often used as a weapon.
Why am I not allowed to fear?
Why does fear have to be a tool?
Why am I never allowed to have my experience?
My voice matters!
Listen to my fear!
I am not here to hurt you!
I am here to show you where you get hurt.
I want to help,
And you ignore me.
Fear and anxiety are important!
You say it almost every work day.
Why are you not allowed to feel it?
Why am I not allowed to be here?
I am so nervous even thinking about speaking up,
How come I don't get a say in choices?
I tell you over and over,
Instead of listening you bury or silence me!
I guess before we discuss the rape,
I need assurances that I will be heard.
I don't need a fancy cape,
I don't need to be catalogued like a bird. I just need to feel seen,
And it is scary bringing this up.
But you all have yet to be mean,
So, I will drink from this cup.
I guess part of the fear,
Is that people will remove my humanity again.
I can intellectually know its progress they'll cheer,
And yet still lie among defeated men.

I still remember what it was like,
To be a sex toy and nothing else.
Lying there, no better than a spike.
Somehow I wanted it, like some sick piece of prose.
As though I derived from it my identity.
I am much more than that,
But I fear getting nothing but pity.
I fear getting caught in depression and getting fat.
Am I still defining myself that way?
Do I have anything that matters to say?
Will there always be damages to pay?
Will my soul always be a game to play?
I guess I know I am better,
But my worries hold me fast like a fetter.
So, what is my next step?
My friends have proven to be safe,
And honestly, it's nice to have none left that are unsafe.
That's why I didn't delay his pep.
He regularly hurt me,
Now he's gone.
That's nice to see.
The death of my last long con.
So what do I need?
To speak openly.
To be heard.
I want people to hear my own word,
And take action instead of using logic to silence me.
To maintain my humanity, I need to advocate for my fear and anxiety with great greed.

THE AWAKENING

The relief I feel is so delightful,
I feel energized.
The way a man who thought we were brothers treated me was frightful.
It was with nagging that he baptized,
And with ruthlessness he kept people bowing.
I am happy to finally admit these things,
As before I would be cowing.
I am allowed out and handed freedom!
Now I get to choose what my life brings.
No more silence.
Because silence is dumb,
And because I'm genuinely free.
Free even with words to mince!
Minced words is my favourite dish,
Such that I am filled with glee!
I have been through a lot,
So much that I'd drown were I not a fish.
I get thrown a lot of shame,
Even I make me feel like a sot.
That I enjoyed what was done to me is confusing,
But I was learning all the same.
I knew it was wrong,
And hated that I found it amusing.

And it wasn't until it stopped that I realized,
But by then, had already sounded, did the gong.
I had become what I despised.
I buried my innocence and joy,
And threw on a mask, a cruel reminder of what had been done,
But today is a new chapter, a new day, and with it,
Comes the sun.

THE MISSING LINK

I feel as though I found the missing link.
I fought against this for so long?
I've perhaps been ambitious in the wrong ways, I think.
I set idealized goals built like a loud gong,
Rather than realistic milestones.
I am happy to be ambitious,
But I was pushing so hard I felt it in my bones.
I think I should set goals that are bite-sized and delicious.
This nameless piece of my soul,
A missing lynch pin of connection.
In her lies much of my mental health goal.
Kind, caring, forward thinking, sassy, flirty, all with great reflection.
This missing part connects the disparate parts of me,
Granting access to skills new and old,
All while dancing, making trouble, and filled with glee.
While my body aches, my soul feels all shiny like gold.
Now to give me the love and attention I need,
As I can't thrive without guarding my rest with greed.

MY DILEMMA

It is interesting to think about,
That I could have suffered so much.
Honestly, I'm shocked I ever came in clutch,
Or that I can even build clout.
But I do these things,
Like, a lot.
Despite the pain, despite the suffering,
I couldn't' let myself be a sot.
I think being open is a good step,
And I am on the fence about confrontation.
I worry that it will be a large conflagration,
And in the aftermath, I will lose family and rep.
Perhaps this is a silly worry,
But it is a worry nonetheless.
And my family will always choose family,
And they are family like me in this mess,
I am not confident about the outcome.
I guess I fear them not believing,
Or worse, believing and not caring,
Or worst of all, believing and siding with them for some reason.
I know those are fears,
And the reality will likely be some middle ground.
But that hasn't stopped the tears,
And it hasn't let me sleep sound.

I guess I wonder if I need to confront them,
Or if I could live and ignore them.
Could I be satisfied in the knowledge that they are free,
And just continue to focus and work on me?

REBIRTH IN MOONLIGHT

I have been so angry for so long,
It is hard to know anything else.
I don't think that being angry is wrong,
It just makes my other feelings wince.
I have so little to be angry about these days,
And I just want to feel like I should.
But this new path wanders through the sun's rays,
And I feel like I could achieve anything I could,
And more besides.
I guess I am tired,
And I don't want to give up the fight.
I know I haven't yet tried,
And I know that I don't want to lose my ire,
But in this new life I don't need to fight to feel right.
I can love freely,
And stress openly.
I can dance when I want,
Without Judgement's haunt.
It's almost as if I've made it,
But I am afraid to say it.
History has taught me not to trust the good,
And fear the light.
I would be a being of darkness if I could,
Because then it's the light I could fight.

It is almost harder to walk in the sun,
As it burns everything it sees.
Perhaps in the moon this belief could be undone,
A pale reflection of the wrath and rocky seas.
Is this my destiny?
I am unused to it being allowed.
I move forward even on bended knee,
Where before I would hide in fear of being followed.
All that is against me on this road is my past,
The trappings of a life held in bondage.
Perhaps that history's hold on me should breathe its last,
And eventually I won't have old wounds freshly bandaged.
Perhaps it is time my watch ended,
And I pursue the life I want fully.
No more leaving the hearth heavily defended,
The time is now to furnish it warmly and not sully.
Calmness and gentleness lead to peace,
And fights should be a last resort.
This is a great time to renew my life's lease,
And keep to a minimum, my vitriolic retort.
I will begin the path tonight,
And while I will stumble,
Please call me Moonlight.
I make no promises not to fumble,
But I do promise to give it my all and try.
For now, I will enjoy this life and sigh.

CHAPTER 27: PEACE

I've solidly entered a new chapter.
I suppose it is high time I re-evaluate things.
It seems poverty is no longer my captor,
And my hearth has some new people socializing.
I guess I need to go over the budget,
And check in on the goals.
Such that my life won't smudge it,
And I'll remain free of holes.

THE NEW, BUT OLD DILEMMA

See, I could just not talk about it,
Shut down and hide like always.
Even thinking about processing it hurts like popping a zit.
I suppose if I hide, the fear stays.
But I don't want to talk about it.
I want to pretend it didn't happen, like always.
It doesn't matter that it sits on my soul like a zit,
Because it eats away at me the longer it stays.
The concept that they could have done more if I talk about it,
Scares me more, because I just thought about me like always.
They could have hurt others and I could share this zit.
The longer I am silent, the longer the potential pain stays.
I also fear what my family will think if I talk abut it.
Will they side against me, like always?
Will they say it is in my head and a natural zit?
I won't know until I talk, but still the fear stays.
Could I handle losing them if I talk about it?
Could I stick to my morals about how I'm treated, like always?
And extricate my family, as I pop this zit?
I could probably do it, but I know my love stays.
How would I even talk about it?
Would I walk in, loud and proud, as always?
Would I be able to do that as I am self-conscious about this zit?
I've never doubted their love before, but that doubt stays.

I want to take time and not be ashamed of it.
I want to ease the fear before entering the pit.
I should set a date to make my plays,
Such that I will be prepared for days.

THE CONFRONTATION

I am afraid.
Easy as that.
How will the emotionally unregulated react to the price I paid?
Probably an explosion, nice and fat.
Do I go one by one?
Do I take my time?
Or do I tell everyone?
And do it in rhyme?
Fear,
It fills me.
Much like a coffee whose flavour brings a tear,
The reality is a lot to see.
I fear the lack of stability,
And the piercing uncertainty.
The unpredictability,
The scalding hot spilled tea.
Liar.
An accusation.
One that would cast me to the fire,
That would make me abandon my station.
Underlying it all,
That is the content of my fear,

I've been treated so poorly for so long I want to change that this fall,
But I fear them tossing me on the grill to sear.
There's more,
But that's enough for now from my store.

THIS ISN'T OVER

It doesn't affect you,
So you don't see it.
A silent cry most fit.
They shout in the streets "me too!"
And all you worry about is how it affects what you do.
Their cries fall on deaf ears that to medicine did commit,
And now their silence deafens with wrists slit.
Meanwhile you say they go too far in the justice they pursue.
Daily I fight to dismantle the lies of this patriarchy,
One by one spreading truth to those who enter my office.
Yet in the silent backdrop you undermine me to save your plutarchy.
Your gentle voice and quiet demeaner letting them think nothing is amiss,
As you destroy the foundation of their confidence until it is they themselves they dismiss.
You claim to seek order, yet all you do is sow anarchy.
Now the voice of the oppressed cry out in unison,
And you wonder why it is that they fight.
"They already had their rallies and marches, right?"
You ask as you step back, tired now you've had your fun.
Your privilege blinds you to the real fight under the sun,
You marched in one march and read one article and found the light?

To you this fight is a fad and done when out of sight,
Yet it won't be until humanity is equal that we are done.
I should say, just to be clear,
That there is nothing wrong with resting,
We are fighting a system; dismantling what those in power hold dear.
It will take time, it will take energy. It is our will they are testing.
And we will stand and show them that they are the ones left wanting.
I know this feels hopeless, but it is our very hope that they fear.

RE-EVALUATING JOY

Excitement is for dumb people and children.
How is that one of my values?
By that definition, all of humanity belongs in the dumb bin.
There is a problem with these views.
So, what to do about it?
Can we change and make better values fit?
I mean, I get to choose the shape I will be,
This transitive time gives me plenty of space,
And plenty of time to discover me.
It is hard to understand that life isn't a race.
I just need to remember that I have time,
And perhaps begin to express excitement in rhyme.

WHY JOY HAS BEEN DISTANT

My excitement lives in the corner of my soul,
It drives much of what I do.
Yet it is hard to see.
Honestly, it is hard to feel, too.
I've been feeling recently like a block of coal.
Being told that, without joy, I am not good enough.
At least, it feels that way to me.
I feel as though I'm being told I must express it,
Yet I do not like to lie about my feelings.
I feel like my way is rough.
I'm tired but I have to be a happy thing.
I'm feeling like some unsightly zit,
Painful and unwanted.
I feel like a child again,
Those I look up to saying to be happy and show it,
Despite it being out of reach, I must flaunt it.
She shows her face now and then,
But it is in the quiet moments.
And she been out of reach since she was told to be loud.
I understand that hurting me wasn't the intent.
I am still feeling hurt.
I hope that is allowed.

But I felt punished last time for feeling,
As though positive vibes are all that are allowed to be sent.
I guess I feel like my fear was dismissed,
And now I would like to run away into the mist.

TIME AND SPACE

Time and Space.
Two concepts that I find quite foreign,
Yet two concepts I need like a sleeve of aces.
This life is one I barely find space in,
And frequently it is too fast.
I need to apply what I learned early in the pandemic,
And be okay going slow and choosing last.
I think I need a new rule to make this stick.
Perhaps it could be something easy,
Like taking a minimum of a sleep and a poem to see.

FORGIVENESS

I feel like I will be in trouble,
Sometimes it is hard to identify why.
This time I think I found something that causes stress to double.
There is a history of forgiveness not being sticky,
Almost always, young Nat lost forgiveness and had to sigh.
The whole process has left me traumatized,
I often feel that resentment will still reign.
This leaves me feeling quite icky,
And more than a little despised.
Is it okay if I see forgiveness without action as a feign?

HUNTER

Am I the one you seek?
Lines dismissed to feel clean,
Yet bright and shining in the creek.
Is there a passage I have not seen?
What conspires within, I wonder,
As the sun sets over the mountain?
Why is it that you come up from under,
While blood drips slowly from this fountain?
I cannot assume I am safe,
Without some reasonable guarantee.
Perhaps a rule around which we act in strife,
Designed in mind for all our safety.
I don't know about this one;
No killing parts, as it cannot be undone.
Leave room for things like Moonlight's melding and evolution,
With no need for some senseless revolution.

CRISIS FATIGUE

Having a sad day in the aftermath of the upheaval,
Plans gone awry and life strewn everywhere.
I am tired, ragged and just so painfully aware.
I seek safety from this awareness in my sanity's retrieval.
Yet the burden of crisis fatigue feels like too great an evil.
Friends gone and wounded in this deep scare,
Throwing blame around the crisis, so blissfully unaware.
Soon, the winter comes, and with it, the lockdown's revival.
When we will need each other most of all,
Is when we most need to isolate.
To yearn for solidarity yet stuck in our own halls.
I feel a deep helplessness tied to this fate,
Yet I know we will prevail and on the other side, commiserate.
Until then, stand fast my friends, and we may yet see next year's fall.

BREAKING MY HABITS

Long have I suffered in silence,
And in my silence, injured those I love.
Long have I backed down from conflict,
And in backing down, fell to every push or shove.
Long have I watched the horrors unfold,
And in so watching, allowed more horror from up above.
I am done.
No longer will I suffer in silence.
I will shout my defiance in the storms.
No longer will I back down.
I will hold my ground and challenge the norms.
No longer will I sit on the sidelines and watch.
I will rise up and fight until a new world forms.
It is no longer enough to be a passenger in my life;
Now is the time to stand in defiance of this global strife.

THE ONCOMING STORM

I fear the damage that will be caused,
Despite knowing the depth of pain already here.
I want to say that nothing is wrong and keep the conflict paused.
My fear grows as the hour draws near.
I feel like my soul is not ready.
Will any conviction withstand the storm and be enough?
When the tide comes in, will I be steady?
Or will I be shattered and splintered on the bluff?
It is not as though I think I am in the wrong,
And the lines I am seeing remind me of the past.
To approach with a delicate hand would take so long,
I know my resolve would not last.
So, I suppose that this is the best option,
Especially given our lack of progress thus far.
I guess I also fear quite the conflagration,
Given how loud my fawnings are.
Today I will attempt to break this cycle.
I will stand fast, whole and complete.
My resolve will not even wrinkle,
My arguments will be fleet.
It is not for pain that I step into this arena,
But for the love I have for my brother.

It is not to cut him off from the other,
But to deepen the bond before they get caught in the corona.
If I balk here, I cause more damage,
Without this act of kindness, their lives will soon be ruins in
   which they rummage.

RELIEF

I feel such peace with this decision,
Despite knowing it will be met with derision.
I am quite confident that it is the right one,
As what has been said cannot be undone.
To face ideation after such success,
And abused repeatedly, no less.
What other choice could be made?
Especially given the foundation that has been laid?
It will be called extreme,
It will be demonized.
Although that further proves our point, I would deem,
It will not stop us from being dehumanized.
My regular response is to just up and leave,
But that cannot happen when our arms are up the same sleeve.
To offer to cover therapy I see as quite generous,
Where normally I'd leave a message quite cantankerous.
I still believe there will be a lashing out,
Since we are denying them their last bout.
That is why I feel relief,
I couldn't handle more abuse, or at least that is my belief.

PROCESSING CONFLICT

I feel I am a scion of defiance,
Ever dancing that line of right and wrong.
Yet it was not I who first broke the reliance,
Not I who wounded our family.
No, I stood shoulder to shoulder and sounded the gong,
Yet when the toll sounded, I listened.
I accept influence rather intentionally,
Yet I receive flack and get written off as manipulated.
See, manipulation would our demise have hastened,
Influence accepted freely has instead healed the divide.
It is in the hatred of manipulation they have capitulated,
Hurling accusations that we obfuscated.
When in reality we communicate as those neurodiversified.
Their complaints are rooted in ableism,
Their arguments in absurdism,
And their blindness in individualism.
They see accepting influence as being manipulatable,
A toxic belief rooted in fear.
If only we could speak knowing that they would hear,
Instead of knowing that in codependence they think they are
 irrefutable.

THE DEPTH OF STRUGGLE

I honestly don't get it.
I presume they understand the stakes,
Yet they still throw a fit.
I guess people have to make mistakes,
But I just don't like losing friends.
I mean, it is the inevitability of growth,
And they fight no matter the ends.
It feels like they fight to fulfill some ancient oath,
That it is them against the world.
It is that same attitude upon which our banners unfurled.

BALKING AT DANGER

I feel like I often balk as the metal meets the road.
Hard choices scare me.
I know that it is the right choice,
I just worry that I cannot bear the emotional load.
Although, if they were as invested in the friendship as we,
We wouldn't have gotten this far or had to think twice.
I should note that people who care do work.
People who care look for how to move forward.
They do not get caught up in precedent,
They look to see what is being brought in, not give in to their irk.
That these friends are not looking for a way to move onward,
And are instead looking to hold us captive in their tenement,
Is very sad and very telling.
I am afraid to hit send because I think they will be found wanting.

A SHAME

I am a scion of darkness,
A harbinger of strife.
At least, that is what is seen in closeness,
By those with whom I have chosen to share my life.
Truly, I tire of this inconsistency.
I tire of those who say one thing and do another.
I tire of those who ignore influence completely.
It just seems that they outnumber and make me feel other.
Too many refuse to grow,
As though it is a sin to see flaw in their partner.
Despite often complaining like some show,
But no others may voice the opinions for starters?
No sense is made.
Like, I get that their trauma gets them to do it,
Convinces them that they'll regret learning had they not stayed.
As though growth and staying together don't fit.
So misguided,
And surrounded myself with them, I did.

SUCH A SHAME

That went badly.
I don't know that it could have gone any worse.
The say that half the battle is knowing the enemy,
But that felt like watching the friendship go away on a hearse.
Like shit, how did they get there?
Why are we assumed to be judge, jury and executioners?
I feel trapped like a hare.
Nowhere to go like some prisoner.
Spiralling in a confirmation cycle,
While showing she isn't all that we fear.
Still felt like she didn't hear,
Like some hard done to uncle.
I feel like there's no point,
Although that's precisely why we are in this joint.

THE ABUSIVE CYCLE

I feel such anxiety.
It is hard to understand.
Intellectually I knew that this was likely,
But it is one thing to know and another entirely to experience it firsthand.
It is quite revealing that she doesn't know what its wrong.
I'll be honest, I thought that we had communicated that.
And when she got going, she went strong.
Following the expected abusive patterns down to the skewed hat.
Such an odd encounter,
I feel like I am the problem.
Now I also knew that would come and I would flounder.
Of my struggles in the world, she is quite the emblem.
I guess the question becomes, do I take the whole day?
Do I cancel my appointments and find rest?
See, it didn't matter what I had to say,
Or even what I've said, apparently, she and her family know best.
Our issues were stated quite loud and clear,
For her and him to miss that brings me fear.
Where do we go when they don't see our tears?
What do we do when they don't believe their peers?

I guess I am a little mad,
And quite a bit sad.
I feel quite gaslit,
And I don't like it one bit.

THE ROAD AHEAD

The long work continues.
I must unravel this pain,
Seek its root in my darkest hues.
I push past each and every stain,
Cleaning as I go.
Too often I find in the cleaning some fight,
As friends are unhappy to see me low,
And do not realize they are not in the right.
Still, I feel that I may be wrong,
Seeing their pain hurts me.
Knowing that I cannot change their song,
Just that I can move forward more carefully.
Some people just need time,
And perhaps therein they'll notice the grime.
Alas, it is not for me to fix them,
Despite the ache in my soul watching them refuse to let their pain stem.

THE KINDLING OF HOPE

It is a comfort to know,
That after so long,
People still know my song.
I had worried I'd have to let go,
And find others,
As this fight smothers.
Yet truth begins to show,
My reputation speaks,
And I climb to life's peaks.
The pain has been hard to swallow,
Yet now I can rise,
As people don't see me as wearing a disguise.
The drawn-out conflict had brought me low,
So much repeated pain,
I felt like a stain.
The end of this damned tunnel begins to glow.
I feel the rekindling of hope.
I'll guard it this time so they can't give it the rope.

THE BURDEN I BEAR

How is it that pain follows me?
One whose presence changes the world.
It is not that I am a giant, so grand to see,
Just that I can shape the world if my plans unfurled.
Yet with such potential comes risk.
I have been careless with my influence.
I didn't take time as I built this obelisk,
And it has fallen hence.
Perhaps more time is needed,
As the fields are reseeded.
Perhaps I need to be more plain,
Such that a small slip causes less pain.
How could you see all that these hands have wrought,
And think that it has not me who labored in these fields?

THE HARMONY

I find my peace in the rhythms of silence.
The soft crunching of snow on a silent morning.
Echoes deadened by fresh powder march thence,
The large flakes, from the sky are falling.
I seek some kind of destiny,
Yet I am most at home in the harmony.

RESILIENT AND IN COMMAND

I am a scion of the darkness.
My mantle is made of tears and broken dreams.
My life has been littered and strewn with mess,
The very fabric of reality fighting against me, it seems.
Yet here I stand,
Resilient and in command.

Around every corner, another fight.
No respite for the wicked and the weary.
Relentless and endless is this blight,
I can barely see, my eyes so heavy and dreary.
Yet still I stand,
Resilient and in command.

In my wake lie peace and discarded conflict,
An odd mix of those willing to listen and grow together,
And those who believe only their own edict.
The latter doing everything they can to keep me from moving forward.
Yet even still I stand,
Resilient and in command.

What can the world throw at me that I have not already thrown myself?
How can the world hurt me when my self-inflicted wounds cut the deepest?
Once my own greatest enemy, now I stand shoulder to shoulder with my darkest self.
Having embraced the darkness in my soul, I have emerged at my best.
So, until I breathe my last, I will stand,
Resilient and in command.

HAVE I DWELT TOO LONG?

My convictions have faded away,
I was so sure of myself yesterday.
What changed in so short a time?
Will I reignite my fire in rhyme?

Perhaps this malaise and depression,
That cemented me last night in position,
Perhaps it has disarmed me,
And I need to engage it to see.

Do my answers lie on the other side?
The foam is thin and rolled in with the tide.
Perhaps a walk to clear my head,
While chatting with a friend instead.

I deserve a moment's peace,
Before the good tidings cease.

THE BETRAYAL

In my darkest hours, I push away those closest to me.
The safety of their presence becomes my deepest fear.
A lesson learned over a decade of trauma.
A scar so deep as to be near impossible to see.
So hidden I couldn't see it until my twenty-seventh year,
And what tipped me off was all this drama.

I was spiralling and out of control,
Hurting everyone around me.
You and your partner encouraged this poison in my soul,
Adding fuel to a wildfire raging so aggressively.
When I was finally able to come to my senses,
I began to rebuild my damaged relationships.
Every talk we had stopped at arbitrary fences,
And every step to understanding lost and given the slip.

That I somehow understood that I was wrong,
Has made us opposed in this conflict.
After what we've been through, why don't you trust my edict?
In your darkness I was here, yet in mine you left me before long.

BEYOND THE VEIL

Who do I think I am?
Why do I fight these fights?
Do I want to be a lion when I am truly a lamb?
Or do I just need my reason in my sight?
Should I break down why I am doing this?
Such that I can no longer feel this doubt?
To hear the lock hiss,
And know my way out?

THE MOLTEN BEING

I remember the molten visage;
It is seared into my memory,
Demanding that I write a poem about the image.
Not knowing why, I'll still do it happily.

It was a moment of infection,
To turn us into a flaming being.
Causing harm without reflection,
Causing pain without seeing.

Perhaps understanding my importance,
And the damage I can cause,
Was the dream's pertinence.
That, before acting, I should pause.

I should always have that conviction,
That understanding of reason.
Such that when I meet obfuscation,
I am not gaslit into treason.

THE PASSING STORM

I find myself awaiting a storm.
The world around me is calm and clear,
The last storm disappearing on the horizon.
In the soil around me, flowers begin to form.
Yet still, I hide in this shelter, too afraid to cheer.
Should I stay here, the flowers will wither before I could set my eyes on.
I have survived this valley.
I have worked hard to make it through alive, have added more losses to my tally,
Yet it is no fault of mine that their true selves arrived.
Despite this storm, look at all I have achieved.
Despite this ache in my soul, look at all I have done.
I have conquered goals a younger me would not have believed,
And yet still, I hide from the sun.
It is high time I trust this win.
It is high time I lowered my guard.
I've earned the smell of flowers on the wind.
I've a celebration waiting for me for which I have worked damn hard!
This season is why I chose to live,
This season is why I refused to give up.
So, for tonight, and all nights hence, I lift my cup,
To a life worth living and plenty of love to give.

SEIZING MY DESTINY

I feel quite battered and bruised,
Yet serenity fills my soul.
It is not as though I haven't failed, it just has no toll.
Even the pain of realizing I've been used,
It doesn't carry the same sting.
I feel like some relentless force,
Forging forward like some thoroughbred horse,
The future being the only song that I sing.
With my sights set, who could ever stop me?
With each new goal, *when* is the only variable before me.
Ever, my way is forward,
I will seize the destiny before me.
Ever, my path is onward,
For too long have I allowed this destiny to elude me.

I WANT TO BE MORE

I wish I could solve every problem.
I wish I could do more.
I do not want them to suffer.
I don't want to see the world gobble 'em.
My soul is sore.
Today could not have been rougher.
I need peace for my weary soul.
I am too busy.
To stoke this flame, I need more coal.
I need time by the sea.
I need to carve out extra me time.
Such that I have space again to rhyme.

RELENTLESS

It may sound arrogant to say,
The world will be changed because of me.
Yet I am realizing today,
That to suffer anything less would be a disservice. you see,
I clawed my way back into the light,
From the brink of depression and destruction.
There are so many souls still lost in that twilight,
So, I cannot stop until suicide numbers head in a downward direction.

www.ingramcontent.com/pod-product-compliance
Lightning Source LLC
LaVergne TN
LVHW021614080426
835510LV00019B/2574